D1243423

History Makers

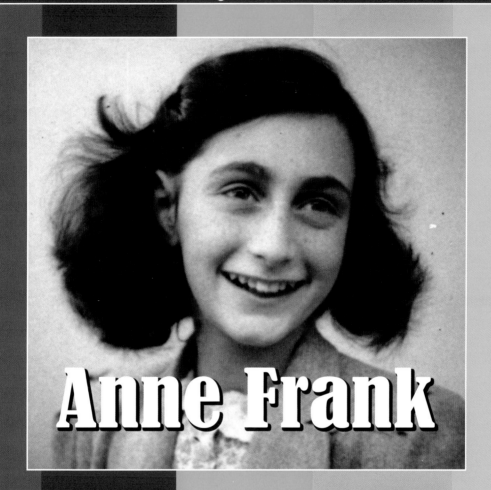

Anne Frank

by Pamela McDowell

www.av2books.com

AV² provides enriched content that supplements and complements this book. Weigl's AV² books strive to create inspired learning and engage young minds in a total learning experience.

Your AV² Media Enhanced books come alive with...

Audio
Listen to sections of the book read aloud.

Key Words
Study vocabulary, and complete a matching word activity.

Video
Watch informative video clips.

Quizzes
Test your knowledge.

Go to **www.av2books.com**, and enter this book's unique code.

BOOK CODE

D 8 0 1 0 1 4

Embedded Weblinks
Gain additional information for research.

Slide Show
View images and captions, and prepare a presentation.

AV² by Weigl brings you media enhanced books that support active learning.

Try This!
Complete activities and hands-on experiments.

... and much, much more!

Published by AV² by Weigl
350 5th Avenue, 59th Floor
New York, NY 10118

Websites: www.av2books.com   www.weigl.com

Library of Congress Cataloging-in-Publication Data

McDowell, Pamela.
 Anne Frank / Pamela McDowell.
   pages cm. -- (Icons: history makers)
 Includes index.
 ISBN 978-1-4896-2456-7 (hardcover : alk. paper) -- ISBN 978-1-4896-2457-4 (softcover : alk. paper) -- ISBN 978-1-4896-2458-1 (single user ebk.) -- ISBN 978-1-4896-2843-5 (multi user ebk.)
 1. Frank, Anne, 1929-1945--Juvenile literature. 2. Jews--Netherlands--Amsterdam--Biography--Juvenile literature. 3. Holocaust, Jewish (1939-1945)--Netherlands--Amsterdam--Biography--Juvenile literature. 4. Amsterdam (Netherlands)--Biography--Juvenile literature. I. Title.
 DS135.N6F73493 2014
 940.53'18092--dc23
 [B]
                                    2014018284

Printed in the United States of America in North Mankato, Minnesota
1 2 3 4 5 6 7 8 9 0 18 17 16 15 14

052014
WEP310514

Editors: Pamela Dell and Heather Kissock
Design: Tammy West

Photograph Credits
Weigl acknowledges Getty Images, Alamy, and iStockphoto as the primary image suppliers for this title. Every reasonable effort has been made to trace ownership and to obtain permission to reprint copyright material. The publishers would be pleased to have any errors or omissions brought to their attention so that they may be corrected in subsequent printings.

Contents

ANNE FRANK and US

"... I'll be able to confide everything to you, as I have never been able to confide in anyone, and I hope you'll be a great source of comfort and support."

Anne Frank

upon receiving her diary on her 13th birthday, June 12, 1942

"Those who deny freedom to others deserve it not for themselves."

Who Was
Anne Frank?

Anne Frank was a young **Jewish** girl. She lived in Amsterdam, the Netherlands, during World War II. At that time, **Nazis** were killing thousands of Jewish people every day. Hoping to escape the Nazis, Anne and her family went into hiding.

The Frank family hid for more than two years. During that time, Anne wrote a diary about her experiences. She recorded events in her life and wrote about the challenges her family faced. When the Nazis discovered the Franks, the family was arrested. Anne left her diary behind. She died in a **concentration camp** seven months later. She was 15 years old.

Anne's diary remained safe. It was published two years after her death. Today, Anne's diary is well-known throughout the world. Both students and adults have read and studied Anne's writings.

Growing Up

Anne was born on June 12, 1929, in Frankfurt, Germany. Her father, Otto, was a banker. Her mother, Edith, took care of their two children. Anne had an older sister, Margot.

In 1933, Adolf Hitler led the Nazis to take control of the German government. Hitler and his government made life very difficult for the Jewish people. Many people left Germany. Anne's family moved to Amsterdam. There, they learned to speak Dutch.

When Anne was almost 11 years old, the Nazis invaded the Netherlands. Anne's life began to change. In 1941, she and Margot were forced to leave their schools. They had to attend a new school that was only for Jewish children. In 1942, the Nazis began sending Jewish people in the Netherlands to labor camps. There was no chance to escape the country. Otto and Edith began making plans to take their family into hiding.

▲ Frankfurt, Germany is home to approximately 700,000 people. It is considered to be the transportation and finance hub of Germany.

Get to Know The
Netherlands

NETHERLANDS

N

SCALE

0   50 Miles

0   50 Kilometers

GERMANY

BELGIUM

> The Netherlands has thousands of windmills. Some are more than 130 feet (40 meters) tall.

> Amsterdam is the capital city of the Netherlands. About 1.5 million people live in the greater Amsterdam area.

> Sometimes the Netherlands is incorrectly called Holland. "Holland" refers to the name of two of the Netherland's provinces. These are North Holland and South Holland.

> There are hundreds of miles of canals in the Netherlands. The North Sea Canal stretches from the North Sea all the way across the country to Amsterdam.

STATE SYMBOLS

COLOR
Orange

ANIMAL
Lion

FLOWER
Tulip

Practice Makes Perfect

On July 5, 1942, Margot received word that she was going to be sent to a German work camp. The next day, the Franks went into hiding. Anne took her schoolbooks and her collection of movie postcards. She also took the red-checkered diary her parents had given her on her 13th birthday. Family friends thought the Franks had gone to Switzerland. Instead, they were hiding in a small apartment hidden behind Otto's office. Anne named it the Secret **Annex**.

The Franks were joined by Hermann and Auguste van Pels and their 15-year-old son Peter. Fritz Pfeffer, a Jewish dentist later joined them. These eight people lived together for more than two years. They never once went outside. A few of Otto's employees brought them food and information about the war.

▲ **The entrance to the annex was covered by a bookcase. The bookcase had hinges so that it could swing back and forth like a door.**

During the day, people were busy in the offices below the Secret Annex. Anne and the others had to be very quiet so that they were not discovered. Anne spent her time sewing and reading. She studied and played board games. She also wrote in her diary.

Anne named her diary "Kitty" and began each entry "Dear Kitty." She wrote about things that happened in the annex. She wrote about growing up and about her hopes and fears for the future. She also wrote short stories.

QUICK FACTS

- Anne loved movies and collected photos and postcards of movie stars.

- Anne's full name was Annelies Marie Frank.

- Anne's father's ancestors had lived in Frankfurt for over 400 years.

- Anne had to leave her cat, Moortje, behind when she went into hiding.

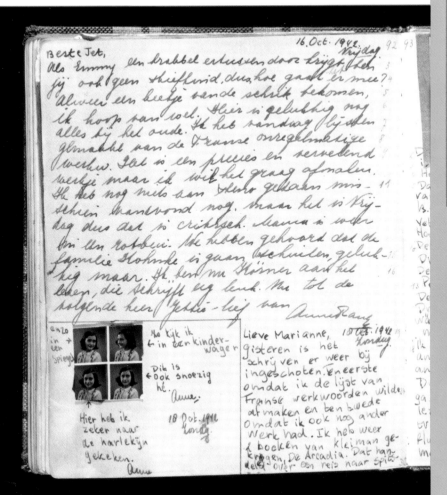

◀ On March 29, 1944, a radio announcer asked people to save their diaries. Anne began to rewrite her work. In 10 weeks, she filled 324 loose pages with her rewrites.

Key Events

While the Franks were in hiding, the news was full of frightening stories. The stories told of Jewish people who went to the Nazi labor camps and never returned. Anne's last diary entry was on August 1, 1944. The Nazis arrived three days later. They arrested everyone in the Secret Annex.

On August 8, Anne and her family were put on a train to Westerbork, a **detention** camp in the Netherland's northeast. There, the Franks were punished for hiding from the Nazis. They were forced to work, taking apart old airplane batteries.

On September 3, 1944, the Franks were put on another train. This time, they were sent to Auschwitz, a death camp in Poland. When the Franks arrived, the men and women were separated. Anne never saw her father again.

▲ An estimated 1.3 million people were sent to Auschwitz. Approximately 85 percent of those people were of Jewish descent.

Thoughts from **Anne**

Anne Frank's diary provides readers with insight into an important time in world history. Her entries reflect the thoughts of a young girl experiencing this time and how she found solace within it.

Anne wrote her first diary entry on June 12, 1942.
"I hope I will be able to confide everything in you, as I have never been able to confide in anyone and I hope you will be a great source of comfort and support."

While in hiding, Anne wrote about finding refuge in her writing.
"When I write, I can shake off all my cares."

On February 3, 1944, Anne wrote about losing hope.
"I've reached the point where I hardly care whether I live or die. The world will keep turning without me, and I can't do anything to change events anyway. I'll just let matters take their course and concentrate on studying and hope that everything will be all right in the end."

In her diary, Anne reflected on the life she had before the war.
"The sun is shining, the sky is deep blue, there's a magnificent breeze, and I'm longing...for everything: conversation, freedom, friends, being alone."

Anne discusses her relationship with her sister in her diary.
"Margot is very kind and would like me to confide in her, but I can't tell her everything. She takes me too seriously, far too seriously, and spends a lot of time thinking about her loony sister, looking at me closely whenever I open my mouth and wondering: is she acting, or does she really mean it?"

On July 15, 1944, Anne wrote about keeping hope.
"It's a wonder I haven't abandoned all my ideals, they seem so absurd and impractical. Yet I cling to them because I still believe, in spite of everything, that people are truly good at heart."

What Is a Diarist?

A diarist is a person who writes about their ideas and experiences. Personal thoughts and feelings are an important part of a diary. Most people use diaries as a way to express their thoughts and feelings on what is happening in their lives.

▲ Diary entries are usually dated. Some diarists include sketches, pictures, or maps along with their written entries.

Most diaries are kept private. Sometimes, however, diaries are published. This usually happens after the writer dies, especially if the diarist has lived through a well-known event or time.

The world can learn much from someone who writes about living through a historical event, a disease, or a disaster. Diarists often write down details about their personal experience that history books might not include.

WRITING ABOUT MEMORIES
People can record their memories in a variety of ways. A diary is a day-by-day record of a person's experiences and thoughts. Diaries are usually very private. Most of the time, they are not meant to be published or even read by others. A memoir is a type of nonfiction book that usually focuses on only part of the author's life. This is different from an autobiography. Like a memoir, an autobiography is the true story of an author's life. However, autobiographies usually tell the story of a person's whole life from its beginning.

Young Writers 101

Lena Mukhina (1925–1991)

Lena Mukhina was a Russian girl who was called the "Anne Frank of Leningrad." Lena began her diary in May 1941. That year, the city of Leningrad was invaded by the Nazis. Lena was 16 years old. The people of Leningrad, now St. Petersburg, had to fight off the Nazis for more than two years. Lena described the deaths of her family, the bombing of the city, and how she survived. Lena stopped writing in her diary in May 1942. She died 49 years later in Moscow. In 2011, Lena's diary was discovered. It was published in Russia under the name *Keep My Sad Story*.

Mattie J.T. Stepanek (1990–2004)

Mattie Stepanek was born in Washington, D.C. He inherited a disease that caused muscle weakness and difficulties with his heart and lungs. Mattie began writing poems in kindergarten. His first book, *Heartsongs*, was published in 2001. He wrote about the need for hope and peace. *Just Peace* is a collection of essays and emails between Mattie and former President Jimmy Carter. That book was published in 2006, after Mattie's death.

Ishmael Beah (1980–)

Ishmael Beah was born in Sierra Leone, a country in Africa. When Ishmael was 12 years old, his family was killed in Sierra Leone's civil war. Ishmael wandered homeless with other young orphans. He was forced to become a child soldier. Ishmael escaped to the United States in 1998. There, he began to write about his experiences. His book, *A Long Way Gone: Memoirs of a Boy Soldier*, was published in 2007.

Melba Pattillo Beals (1941–)

Melba Beals was born in Little Rock, Arkansas. In 1957, Melba became one of the "Little Rock Nine." She and eight other young African American students volunteered to be the first to **integrate** into Little Rock's all-white Central High School. Melba and the other eight students faced violent protesters. A soldier was assigned by the government to protect Melba. She recorded her thoughts and the events of this difficult time in a diary. The book *Warriors Don't Cry*, published in 1994, was based on Melba's diary.

Influences

The two people who had the greatest influence on Anne were her parents. Otto Frank was a calm and thoughtful man. He encouraged his daughters to learn about other religions and would hold **Christian** celebrations, such Easter and Christmas, with his family. Otto also valued education. In the Secret Annex, he tutored his daughters and Peter. He encouraged Anne to write and respected the privacy of her diary.

▲ Anne's parents were married on May 12, 1925. They spent their honeymoon in San Remo, Italy.

Anne's mother was very religious. She followed Judaism more strictly than Otto. Before the Franks went into hiding, Edith attended **synagogue** regularly. She allowed only **kosher** foods. Like many young girls, Anne did not always agree with her mother. In her diary, Anne often wrote about their arguments and her frustrations.

ANNE AND MARGOT

The two Frank sisters, Margot and Anne, were very different from one another. Margot, three years older, was quiet and shy. She was a good student who spent much of her time working on her schoolwork. Anne was chatty and curious. She was full of energy and found it difficult to concentrate at school. While in hiding, Anne had a much harder time staying quiet and still than Margot did. Anne wrote in her diary that she did not understand Margot or confide in her. The sisters supported each other, though, as they were moved from camp to camp.

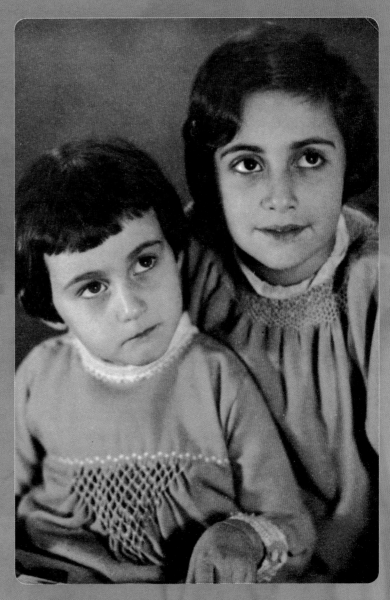

▶ Like Anne, Margot kept a diary while in hiding. Margot's diary was never found.

Overcoming Obstacles

When people arrived at Auschwitz, they were sent on one of two paths. Some people went directly to the **gas chambers**. Others were put to work. Anne was put in the work line. Her head was shaved, and a freezing hut became her new home. For weeks, Anne, Margot, and Edith worked very hard hauling stones and digging grass from a field. Then, in October 1944, Anne and Margot were sent to another camp. Edith remained at Auschwitz. She died there on January 6, 1945.

The Frank sisters arrived together at Bergen-Belsen, in Germany. This was a different kind of death camp. It did not have gas chambers. Instead, people died very slowly of starvation or infectious diseases. Lice were common and caused the spread of **typhus** among the prisoners.

◀ **Auschwitz was heavily guarded, with watchtowers at regular intervals along electrified barbed wire fences.**

Anne and Margot worked each day taking shoes apart. Their hands bled from the difficult work. There was no food or water in their part of the camp. Both Anne and Margot became very ill with typhus.

By March 1945, the sisters were starving and had become very weak. In March 1945, Margo fell from her bunk and died. Anne died a few days later. On April 15, 1945, British soldiers arrived at Bergen-Belsen. The soldiers freed all the prisoners who were still alive.

▶ **Little of Bergen-Belsen remains today. A monument stands on the site to commemorate those who lost their lives at the camp.**

ISRAEL AND THE WORLD SHALL REMEMBER
THIRTY THOUSAND JEWS
EXTERMINATED IN THE CONCENTRATION CAMP
OF BERGEN-BELSEN
AT THE HANDS OF THE MURDEROUS NAZIS

EARTH CONCEAL NOT THE BLOOD
SHED ON THEE!

FIRST ANNIVERSARY

Achievements and Successes

When the Nazis removed Anne and the others from the Secret Annex, they also took the few valuables they found. Anne's diary and her loose pages of writing, however, were left behind. Later, Miep Gies, one of Otto's employees, gathered up all of Anne's writings. She tucked the diary and papers into her desk drawer without reading them.

Eight people had hidden in the annex, but only Otto Frank survived the war. He returned to Amsterdam in June 1945. There, Miep gave him Anne's work. Otto wanted people to know about Anne and her story. He decided to send the diary to a publisher. The diary was published in the Netherlands in 1947. The book sold very quickly.

▲ Anne Frank continues to fascinate people all over the world. Besides her diary, there are now numerous biographies of Anne that provide even more information about her life.

German and French editions were published in 1950. The book came out in the United States and Great Britain in 1952, under the title *The Diary of a Young Girl*. In the 1960s, Anne's book was introduced into American schools.

Today, Anne's diary is known around the world. It has been published in more than 65 languages and has sold more than 30 million copies. On October 5, 1955, *The Diary of Anne Frank* opened as a play in New York City. It won the 1955 Pulitzer Prize for drama as well as many other awards. A film version, **also called** *The Diary of Anne Frank*, opened in March 1959. It was one of the first Hollywood movies to mention the **Holocaust** and the treatment of the Jewish people during World War II. The film received three Academy Awards from Hollywood's Academy of Motion Picture Arts and Sciences.

ANNE FRANK HOUSE

The Secret Annex where Anne hid for two years was nearly torn down to make way for a new building. Otto Frank and his friends begged for help from the people of Amsterdam. The Anne Frank Fond was set up in 1957. Its purpose was to raise money to save the building. The foundation also wanted to highlight Anne's ideas about tolerance and hope. The Anne Frank House opened as a museum in 1960.

▶ Anne's legacy lives on in the Anne Frank House in Amsterdam. In 2013, the museum received more than one million visitors.

Write a Biography

A person's life story can be the subject of a book. This kind of book is called a biography. Biographies describe the lives of remarkable people, such as those who have achieved great success or have done important things to help others. These people may be alive today, or they may have lived many years ago. Reading a biography can help you learn more about a remarkable person.

At school, you might be asked to write a biography. First, decide who you want to write about. You can choose a diarist, such as Anne Frank, or any other person. Then, find out if your library has any books about this person. Learn as much as you can about him or her. Write down the key events in this person's life. What was this person's childhood like? What has he or she accomplished? What are his or her goals? What makes this person special or unusual?

A concept web is a useful research tool. Read the questions in the following concept web. Answer the questions in your notebook. Your answers will help you write a biography.

Your Opinion

- What did you learn from the books you read in your research?
- Would you suggest these books to others?
- Was anything missing from these books?

Childhood

- Where and when was this person born?
- Describe his or her parents, siblings, and friends.
- Did this person grow up in unusual circumstances?

Adulthood

- Where does this individual currently reside?
- Does he or she have a family?

Writing a Biography

Main Accomplishments

- What is this person's life's work?
- Has he or she received awards or recognition for accomplishments?
- How have this person's accomplishments served others?

Work and Preparation

- What was this person's education?
- What was his or her work experience?
- How does this person work. What is or was the process he or she uses or used?

Help and Obstacles

- Did this individual have a positive attitude?
- Did he or she receive help from others?
- Did this person have a mentor?
- Did this person face any hardships?
- If so, how were the hardships overcome?

Timeline

YEAR	ANNE FRANK	WORLD EVENTS
1929	Annelies Marie Frank is born on June 12.	The U.S. stock market crashes in the first disaster of the Great Depression.
1933	Anne begins school in Amsterdam.	Adolf Hitler gains absolute power over Germany on August 2.
1941	Anne and Margot are transferred to a Jewish school after the Nazis invade the Netherlands.	Winston Churchill becomes prime minister of Great Britain.
1941	New anti-Jewish laws forbid Anne from attending movies or using public transportation.	The Japanese attack Pearl Harbor in Hawai'i, and the U.S. enters World War II.
1942	The Frank family goes into hiding.	The Manhattan Project, a secret U.S. project aimed at building the first atomic bomb, begins.
1944	Anne's family is discovered in the Secret Annex and is sent to a detention camp.	**Allied** forces invade Normandy, France, on June 6. This is the first big push to free western Europe from Nazi control.
1945	Anne dies of typhus in Bergen-Belsen concentration camp.	Germany surrenders, ending World War II in Europe.

Key Words

Allied: the countries opposed to Germany during World War II

annex: a smaller building or addition connected to a larger main building

Christian: following the teachings of Jesus Christ

concentration camp: a guarded compound for the confinement of political prisoners or minorities

detention: the act of forcing people to stay somewhere against their will

gas chambers: Nazi-built rooms meant to kill people by making them breathe gas instead of air

Holocaust: the Nazis' systematic killing of millions of Jewish people and others during World War II

integrate: end the separation of African Americans and whites in schools and other places

Jewish: someone or something that belongs to the Jewish religion, or Judaism

kosher: fit to be eaten or used under the laws of Judaism

Nazis: those belonging to an extreme political group formed and led by Adolf Hitler in the 1930s

synagogue: a building for Jewish worship and religious study

typhus: an infectious disease that is transmitted by lice

Index

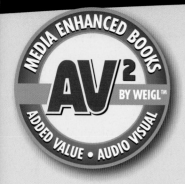

Log on to www.av2books.com

AV² by Weigl brings you media enhanced books that support active learning. Go to www.av2books.com, and enter the special code found on page 2 of this book. You will gain access to enriched and enhanced content that supplements and complements this book. Content includes video, audio, weblinks, quizzes, a slide show, and activities.

AV² Online Navigation

Book Pages
AV² pages directly correspond to pages in the book.

Audio
Listen to sections of the book read aloud.

Video
Watch informative video clips.

Key Words
Study vocabulary, and complete a matching word activity.

Embedded Weblinks
Gain additional information for research.

Quizzes
Test your knowledge.

Slide Show
View images and captions, and prepare a presentation.

Try This!
Complete activities and hands-on experiments.

AV² was built to bridge the gap between print and digital. We encourage you to tell us what you like and what you want to see in the future.

Sign up to be an AV² Ambassador at www.av2books.com/ambassador.

Due to the dynamic nature of the Internet, some of the URLs and activities provided as part of AV² by Weigl may have changed or ceased to exist. AV² by Weigl accepts no responsibility for any such changes. All media enhanced books are regularly monitored to update addresses and sites in a timely manner. Contact AV² by Weigl at 1-866-649-3445 or av2books@weigl.com with any questions, comments, or feedback.